Original title:

Ivy in the Shadows

Copyright © 2025 Creative Arts Management OÜ
All rights reserved.

Author: Wyatt Kensington
ISBN HARDBACK: 978-1-80581-783-3
ISBN PAPERBACK: 978-1-80581-310-1
ISBN EBOOK: 978-1-80581-783-3

Growth Under Wraps

In a corner, creeping sly,
A plant with dreams to touch the sky.
It wiggles here and dances there,
With leaves that tickle, light as air.

In the dark, it throws a show,
Doing cartwheels, stealing the glow.
Whispering secrets to the night,
A leafy prankster, full of light.

With a twist and sneak, it makes a mess,
Hiding in corners, quite the dress!
A game of peek-a-boo it plays,
Flirting with shadows, in leafy displays.

It wraps around, a playful tease,
Inviting giggles in the breeze.
So when you see it, don't you grin,
Just know the fun is about to begin!

The Hidden Heart of the Forest

In the dappled light, a bunny leaps,
While the old oak tree silently peeps.
A squirrel does ballet on a branch,
With acorn dreams, they take their chance.

Tiny mushrooms wear hats so grand,
Join the dance with a fairy band.
Beneath the ferns, a fox does grin,
While giggling beetles scurry in.

Entwined in Darkness

A raccoon plays hide and seek at night,
With a moonbeam that shines just right.
In a tangle of leaves, they'll stumble,
Tripping over roots with a humorous tumble.

The owls hoot laughter, wise and bright,
While creatures plot their sneaky flight.
All the shadows join the game,
As laughter echoes, wild and tame.

A Ballet of Twilit Leaves

Leaves twirl gently, a graceful prance,
As crickets chirp in their evening dance.
A hedgehog whispers, "Don't let them hear,"
But a dancing twig rolls with cheer.

The night air bubbles with critters' glee,
Who knew a forest could be so free?
With every rustle, mischief unfolds,
In the quiet corners, a tale retold.

Shadows Wrapped in Greenery

A turtle wears shades, cool as a brook,
While squirrels read maps, with a secret nook.
A snake tries to slither, stumbles and twists,
Creating a riddle that none can resist.

With shadows that giggle, they whisper and plot,
A game of charades in this leafy spot.
The forest erupts with laughter so bright,
As critters unite in this joyful night.

The Nature of Secrets

In the garden, whispers grow,
Leaves giggle, when winds blow.
A vine with secrets, bows in grace,
Winks at the sun, with a playful face.

Funny how the shadows speak,
In twirls and twists, they hide and peek.
A world alive, with laughter echoing,
Foliage grins, as the secrets are growing.

Beneath the Silent Canopy

Underneath a leafy shroud,
Where laughter hides, beneath a crowd.
Gnarled roots with stories rare,
Tickle the toes, without a care.

Branches sway, in a giggling dance,
Nature's jest in a leafy trance.
Who knew the trees had so much to say?
With twigs and branches leading the way.

Enigma of the Climber

A little sprout with dreams to reach,
Climbs up high, avoiding the breach.
Poking fun at the world down there,
As if it's shouting, 'Do you dare?'

With each twist, it gains a grin,
Outsmarting critters, it wears a spin.
Nature's acrobat, cheeky and spry,
Under the sun's gaze, it aims for the sky.

The Elusive Shadows

Sneaky figures dance at dusk,
Playing hide-and-seek, with a funky musk.
Rustling leaves like giggling kids,
Creating mischief where silence bids.

Oh, the fun, the games they play,
Patterns shifting, come what may.
In curious forms, they tease and flee,
These shadows know, how wild life can be!

The Lurkers of Twilight

In corners deep, they stretch and sway,
Green tendrils dance at close of day.
With mischief stitched in every vine,
They giggle soft, their jokes benign.

They peek from cracks, behind the wall,
In moonlight's glow, they have a ball.
Whispered pranks in nighttime air,
To tickle fright—oh, do they dare!

Serpentine Echoes of the Past

Old stories twist in leafy curls,
Of secret loves and hidden pearls.
With every twist and turn, they tease,
Their laughter hides amongst the trees.

What did you say? Oh, speak it clear!
Their antics spark both joy and fear.
In sap and bark, legends reside,
A past so twisty, hard to bide.

Amongst the Echoing Leaves

The leaves chuckle when no one's near,
In rustles soft, they spread good cheer.
They natter on in breezy jest,
As shadows dance, they're feeling blessed.

A little nibble here and there,
They stash the crumbs without a care.
With tiny giggles on the breeze,
They play their games amongst the trees.

Where Secrets Creep

Beneath the boughs, where shadows dwell,
They plot and plan, their mischief swell.
With winks and nudges, they convene,
In secret schemes, they're quite the scene.

They whisper tales that twine and wind,
Of all the folly left behind.
In creeping vines that play the part,
They spin their webs, oh, so smart!

Trails of the Unseen

In the corners, creeping low,
A band of leaves puts on a show.
They giggle and dance without a care,
In sneakers made of sun-kissed air.

Beneath the fence, they take a peek,
Swaying gently, playing hide and seek.
They chuckle softly, sharing a joke,
As mister squirrel gives a thoughtful poke.

A friendly breeze gives them a spin,
Drawing laughter from deep within.
With whispers sweet and mischief rife,
They lead the way to a leafy life.

Whispers in the Verdant

A rustle here, a giggle there,
The leaves converse without a care.
They share tales of the rain and sun,
As if their fun has just begun.

In the garden, a secret spree,
In vibrant hues, where all is free.
They trade rumors of passing bugs,
And plan to snag a few more hugs.

With roots entwined in playful knots,
They twist and turn in lively spots.
Every flutter, a cheeky tease,
In the heart of green, they aim to please.

The Hidden Bower

Beneath the boughs, a laughter trail,
With leafy caps and giggly veil.
They spin around with not a care,
While dandelions toss in the air.

The sun-drenched spots, their favorite stage,
Where each little leaf feels like a sage.
They pop out laughing from their lair,
Secretive smiles everywhere!

Like tiny jesters on a quest,
In this green corner, they are blessed.
Whirling joy in nature's own way,
With every rustle, they enjoy the play.

The Leafy Veil

Behind the wall, the gremlins scheme,
In leafy cloaks, they plot and dream.
With a wink and a soft chuckle low,
They plan a dance, and off they go!

They tumble forth with mirthful looks,
In playful jests, like storybooks.
They leap and twist, and spin about,
As sunbeams burst, they scream and shout!

From hedges deep, their laughter flies,
With only shadows as their ties.
Yet joy is seen in every shade,
A leafy band, where fun is made.

The Green Veil of the Forgotten

Once tangled whispers giggled low,
Beneath a vine where no sun would go.
A playful dance, a secret pact,
Where shadows blend and laughter's packed.

Leaves chuckle softly at the prying eyes,
Winking, blinking, amid the surprise.
A green disguise, a cloak so clever,
Bouncing jokes that last forever.

Clusters of Enchantment

In the twisty maze, a joker hides,
Witty as the moon while the world abides.
Little greens with smirks and glee,
Playing tag where no one can see.

Beneath the boughs, a comedy show,
Lurking giggles, stealing the glow.
Sprightly vines weave tales of the sly,
With puns that dangle, oh my, oh my!

Echoes from the Understory

From leafy depths, a chuckle creeps,
Where light barely flirts and mischief leaps.
Tumbling stories of joy unfold,
Curly tendrils of green, bold and cold.

The shadows squeal with laughter bright,
As playful sprouts make jokes at night.
A rollicking hymn from roots below,
With every quirk, the undergrowth glows.

Lurking Tangles of Time

Twisted strands that weave a tale,
Of capers gone awry, without fail.
A jester's grin in the leaf's embrace,
In laughter's hold holds a tricky space.

Around each turn, a punchline waits,
With nature's humor that never abates.
Tangled times where mischief grows,
In green-draped corners, frolic flows.

Lurking in the Gloom

In the corner, something stirs,
A giggle, then a flurry of furs.
Behind the pot, a sneaky glance,
Who knew that plants could dance?

A leaf with feet, it makes a leap,
Then hides away without a peep.
Whispers from the dusty air,
"Did you see? No time to care!"

Mischief blooms as shadows talk,
A vine that loves to take a walk.
With every rustle, a new prank plays,
To brighten up the gloomy days!

Oh, the tales that silence keeps,
Of creeping greens and secret peeps.
In laughter, tiny roots would play,
While night cloaks them, come what may!

The Covert Serpent

Underneath the garden gate,
A wiggly form that's hard to state.
Sneaking round with clever grace,
Is that a vine or a playful case?

With a twist and subtle sway,
It tickles heels in a sneaky way.
All the bots are unaware,
Of the green craft hiding there.

Under moonlight, mischief grows,
In whispers, the green serpent knows.
It coils 'round chairs, gives a fright,
And giggles at the silly sight!

As daylight comes, it slips away,
Leaves no trace of last night's play.
Yet in the dark, the joke still thrives,
Where greenery comes alive with jives!

Veined in Darkness

Creeping 'neath the fence's edge,
A vine with antics, bold, a pledge.
With every rustle, a giggle plays,
While shadows dance in silly ways.

A prankster dressed in leafy wraps,
It takes the form of funny laps.
With every twist and stealthy stride,
A green comedian trying to hide.

It tickles toes, it sways on high,
Underneath the starlit sky.
With secret laughs and leafy glee,
Bringing silliness to you and me!

Oh, the tales that vine could tell,
Of nighttime frolics and giggles bell.
In soft embrace of the night it clings,
A whisper of nonsense as laughter sings!

An Unseen Grasp

In the quiet corner, something waits,
An unseen grasp that jests and prates.
Leaves that linger, tendrils sneak,
Through laughter loud, they softly peak.

With a wiggle and a zany curl,
It wraps around to make you twirl.
An uproarious dance beneath the stars,
Where stealthy greens turn into czars.

A poke and pinch from vines so spry,
They twine and twist while you comply.
But watch your step, they tease and tease,
With every move, they do as they please!

In shadows thick, they spread the cheer,
In every rustle, a laugh draws near.
So if you find a sneaky sprout,
Just join the dance, there's fun about!

The Silent Watchers Beneath

Beneath the boughs, they quietly giggle,
As the squirrels play tag and trees wiggle.
With leaves like hats and roots for shoes,
They've mastered the art of sneaky blues.

A raccoon winks as it sneaks a snack,
While owls exchange jokes, not a single quack.
Branches sway with mysterious grace,
Nature's secret, a lively space!

Enchanted Foliage at Dusk

At dusk, the leaves begin to dance,
Mischief brews in their leafy prance.
The moon is a stage for shadows to play,
Twilight's comedians, in a leafy cabaret!

Witty vines twist and tangle tight,
Tickling the paths in the fading light.
Crickets chirp their nightly tunes,
While fireflies wink at those silly goons!

Nature's Quiet Entanglement

In a tangle of greens, a secret parade,
Whispering trees, their jokes never fade.
A beetle staggers, a comic little chap,
While twigs chuckle softly as they overlap.

Petals snicker and share sly grins,
While a rustling breeze spins tales of wins.
Nature's odd blend of chaos and cheer,
Creating laughter for all those who hear!

Veins of Darkness and Light

In the spaces where shadows play peek,
The sunlight giggles, a warm little squeak.
With roots in the earth and leaves up high,
They tickle the edges of the watchful sky.

Twisting and turning, the branches engage,
A merry little show upon nature's stage.
As dusk melts softly into night's delight,
The jokes of the woods bring a smile so bright!

Beneath the Canopy

Underneath the leafy grin,
Squirrels plot their little win.
Hiding snacks with crafty flair,
Giggles float upon the air.

Beneath the beams of dappled light,
A snail races, what a sight!
Chasing shadows, quick and sly,
As butterflies wave bye-bye.

Nature's Quiet Intrigue

In the hush, a whispered joke,
Frogs in tuxedos, oh what a bloke!
They croak the punchlines, loud and clear,
While fireflies dance, a charmed sphere.

The trees lean close, they cannot wait,
For antics that they celebrate.
Banter flows through bamboo sprees,
As red ants hum their melodies.

Hidden Amongst the Leaves

A raccoon with a mask so black,
Steals the snacks and makes a jibe,
Whispers softly, 'What a hack!'
While birds chirp gossip, taking bribe.

A lizard lounges, claims the sun,
Brags about his latest run.
The trees all snicker, what a tease,
As critters dance with utmost ease.

The Enigmatic Clutch

Among the vines, a secret crew,
Host a party, just a few.
With acorns raised, they toast the day,
As hedgehogs dance in their own way.

Mice in capes, they spin and twirl,
Join the fun, give it a whirl!
Echoes of laughter fill the glen,
Nature's jesters jump again!

Secrets in the Thicket

In the garden, whispers bloom,
A plant with secrets, causing gloom.
It stretches far, it spreads with glee,
A leafy prankster, can't you see?

Behind the fence, it skitters sly,
It tickles toes as we walk by.
With every twist, it dares to tease,
A green comedian among the trees.

Moonlit Tangles

Beneath the moon, it finds its way,
Dancing vines at the end of day.
It creaks and groans, a spooky jest,
Yet wraps around, it's quite the guest.

With a laugh, it pulls, it tugs,
And steals the warmth from cozy rugs.
In shadows deep, it takes a bow,
This jester plant, oh, what a show!

A Haunting Embrace

In the night, it creeps and crawls,
Brushing gently against the walls.
A ghostly touch, yet soft and sly,
It holds you close, oh my, oh my!

Tickle and tease, a playful ghost,
In every corner, it loves the most.
With leaves aglow, it makes us grin,
A haunted hug where fun begins.

The Silent Climber

Quietly creeping, it claims the space,
With a smirk, it keeps its pace.
No sound is made, yet mischief's near,
A stand-up plant without a fear.

Up the trellis, it takes a ride,
With tiny leaves, it beams with pride.
In every nook, it plays its role,
A silent climber, pure comedy soul.

Areas of Concealment

In corners where light fails to play,
A fig leaf's costume for a leafy ballet.
Lurking with giggles, the greens take a chance,
Concealing their antics in a shadowy dance.

A pot with a plant that's a real hoot,
Wearing a hat, for it's far from mute.
Whispers of mischief when nobody's near,
The vines share their jokes with no worries or fear.

The Gloomy Embrace

In the dark corners where whispers reside,
A frown from a fern is some leafy pride.
The moss snickers softly at secrets it keeps,
While moonlight tickles the dirt as it sleeps.

A tumbleweed rolls in with a comedic flair,
Joking with roots, a light-hearted affair.
Darkness can't catch them, the laughter's too bright,
They relish the night with cheerful delight.

Woven Whispers of Life

A tangle of leaves tips its hat to the breeze,
Tickled by secrets that wiggle with ease.
The garden's a chatterbox, tales all around,
As petals burst laughing without making a sound.

Mischief in greens, playing hide and seek,
With vines that are crafty, though innocently meek.
Grapevines drink tea while the daisies confide,
In a party of plants that bloom side by side.

A Tangle of Secrets

What's peeking from behind that old wall?
A dandelion dressed up for the ball!
Shadows keep giggling, it's a marvelous show,
With a curtain of leaves making quite the tableau.

The little ones tumble, avoiding the light,
Chasing each other, they giggle in flight.
In hidden nooks where no one can see,
A riot of laughter flows carefree and free.

The Living Shroud

In corners, life begins to creep,
With leafy gossip, secrets keep.
They woo the wall, with a sly wink,
While giggles of nature softly wink.

A coat of green, a sneaky guise,
Hiding all in playful lies.
With each twist and sly entreat,
They dance about with stealthy feet.

The sun might shine, but they're no fool,
In shades they flourish, joy's own school.
A living blanket, snug and tight,
Tickling toes in morning light.

When breezes blow, they shimmy fast,
The outdoor party, never last.
In merry mischief all around,
In silent laughter, joy is found.

Nature's Quiet Watchers

In the stillness, hidden eyes,
Peeking through a leafy disguise.
Whispered laughs in the gentle breeze,
Nature's guardians take their ease.

Behind the ferns, a wink is tossed,
Amongst the blooms, a laughter lost.
These quiet watchers, oh so sly,
Catching silliness that floats by.

With every rustle, they conspire,
A gentle nudge, a secret fire.
As the world rushes all around,
Their chuckles echo, soft and sound.

In their realm of blissful cheer,
Nature's jesters, ever near.
In the shade, they find their fun,
Rolling invisibly, just begun.

Enveloping Embrace

Silently wrapping, a soft caress,
A verdant hug, no need to dress.
They hold the world in a joking grasp,
Tickling trunks, a humorous clasp.

Around the trees, they twist and twine,
Whispers of green, oh how they shine.
An embrace of laughter, wild and free,
In every nook, pure glee we see.

Nature's secret, a twist of fate,
With tendrils of jest, they play, create.
In playful shrouds, they hide the glee,
Inviting all for a joyful spree.

Come, join the fun in the leafy maze,
In wraps of laughter, we'll all stay ablaze.
For in this shroud of whimsy and flair,
Nature's humor is everywhere.

Tendrils of Invisibility

A creeping mischief on silent feet,
Where laughter dances, oh so sweet.
With sneaky tendrils, they weave their spell,
Invisible giggles, you know it well.

Hugging the path, they prance and play,
In the shade where shadows sway.
A game of peek-a-boo, so sly,
More fun than a pie thrown in the sky.

In a twist of green, silliness grows,
Wit wrapped tight, it subtly flows.
Tendrils tickling with each breeze,
Nature's jesters, eager to tease.

So if you wander through this green,
Be wary of what might be seen.
For in the mist of their playful art,
Lies the jesting joy of nature's heart.

Tendrils of Time

In a garden where whispers play,
A vine dances, leading astray.
With nimble feet, it climbs so high,
As squirrels point up, 'Oh my, oh my!'

A clock ticks loud on the old oak tree,
While leaves laugh, 'Time is not for thee!'
With a tug on a hat and a cheeky grin,
That sneaky plant steals the show again.

It wraps up the gate and plays peek-a-boo,
With a wink and a twirl, it knows just what to do.
Garden gnomes chuckle at its clever schemes,
In the sunlight, it spins, fulfilling its dreams.

Yet when night falls, with a mischievous gleam,
It sways to the rhythm of a grasshopper's dream.
While shadows giggle and the moon takes its throne,
The garden is alive, and the vine's not alone!

Beneath the Cloak of Green

Beneath coats of emerald, things come alive,
With critters and giggles, oh how they thrive!
A butterfly sneezes; the flowers all shout,
In this secret hideout, a ticklish bout.

The snail wears a hat that's far too wide,
With a swagger so cool, it takes a ride.
While worms throw a party, all squirmy inside,
A ruckus erupts from the home they won't hide.

Every breeze carries laughter, a mirthful tune,
As shadows get playful under the moon.
With a jolly old frog singing a blubbery song,
Nature joins in, nodding all along!

So if you should wander where silliness glows,
Just peek through the green; you'll see how it flows.
With giggles and wiggles, the night comes alive,
Amongst all the wonders, oh how they thrive!

The Subtle Intruder

A sly little vine tiptoes in soft,
With quirky tendrils like hands, oh so oft!
Inviting more chaos with each little creep,
As it finds cozy spots where it can leap.

Fairies in laughter throw shade at its games,
While it sneaks past the gnomes, who call out their names.
With a flip and a flop, it climbs with a cheer,
Announcing to all, 'Let's party down here!'

It playfully nibbles on toes of the toad,
As squirrels look on, sharing snacks on the road.
But who'll tell the tale of the night gone undone?
When an intruder's fun is measured in sun!

So next time you find a little green band,
Know it's in the mix, a comical stand.
With chuckles and whispers, it runs all around,
A subtle intruder, dancing unbound!

Shadows of the Evergreen

In the cool of the dusk, shadows start to sway,
Beneath leafy noses, secrets play.
A squirrel with glasses reads tales from the bark,
While the shadows dance wildly, leaving their mark.

Beneath boughs of green, mischief brews hot,
With giggles and whispers filling the plot.
A lizard in bowtie ensures there's a show,
As the stars blink awake, and the moon starts to glow.

With fireflies zipping like ribbons of light,
The laughter erupts, 'What a magical night!'
Beneath every shadow, new stories unfold,
As the sprites share their gossip, both silly and bold.

So let's dance through the green where laughter is found,
Hear the songs of the shadows that spin round and round.
In the heart of the night, there's always a chance,
When spirits are merry, it's time to dance!

Nature's Cloaked Heart

In the garden, whispers play,
Foliage dances night and day.
A leaf dressed up in denim blue,
Guess what? It's the tree's debut!

Squirrels giggle, underbark,
Playing tag until it's dark.
Rabbits hop, their tails a blur,
Who knew nature could confer?

Roots entangle, secrets speak,
Plants wear shades, so very chic.
A helm of moss upon a stone,
Crowned royals in the green unknown.

Wiggling worms throw a grand ball,
Beneath the ferns, we're having a ball.
Nature laughs, her heart so spry,
In leafy realms, the jokes fly high!

In the Grip of Greens

Clovers in a funny fight,
Tickling toes left and right.
Thorns whisper, 'Take a chance!'
In this wild, we laugh and dance.

Lizards wear their emerald coats,
And gossip like old goats.
Each tendril twists, a giggling spree,
As bees buzz tunes of jubilee.

Fungi peep out, quite the show,
Mushroom caps in a duo, show.
Funky roots throw crazy parties,
While owls snicker at their smarties.

Vines may climb, but they are sly,
Poking fun from way up high.
In this jungle, with a twist,
Laughter echoes, can't resist!

The Cryptic Vine

Up the fence, a vine so sly,
Hiding secrets, not a lie.
It beckons whispers in the breeze,
"Oh, come and find what you may seize!"

Bumblebees don shades of green,
Endless jesters, quite the scene.
A lizard grins, adjusts his tie,
An ivy ball, oh my, oh my!

Branches sway with a wink and nod,
Roots are tangled, quite the clod.
Nature's laughter, never stiff,
His wayward curls are so adrift.

Each twist and turn, a riddle made,
In this thicket, fears allayed.
Join the fun, let's take a dive,
In this wild, we feel alive!

Shrouded in Growth

A patch of green, who hides beneath?
A little secret, or a thief?
Leaves are laughing, playing peek,
As the shadows start to speak.

Beneath the bramble, creatures cheer,
In the thicket, never fear.
Mice wear hats, with tails so grand,
A woodland party, quite unplanned!

Weeds wear costumes, all in style,
They dance around with cheeky guile.
Nature's pranks are oh so sly,
In this green room, we all comply.

As the sun dips down, we'll sing,
Join the jam, let's do our thing.
What a sight, this merry grove,
With giggles wrapped in leafy cove!

Tracks Beneath the Shade

In a garden where giggles grow,
A sneaky vine steals the show.
With whispered tricks and leafy schemes,
It dances round in leafy dreams.

A cat in search of a sunny spot,
Trips on strands that twist and knot.
He swears it's a monster that he can't see,
But it's just that plant, and a bee.

Birds chirp tales of this merry green,
That ties up feet, what a sight to glean!
With every step, a little surprise,
A playful twist beneath sunny skies.

So if you stroll beneath the leaves,
Beware of the fun the green one weaves.
For in those shadows, laughter sways,
Catch a giggle, in playful ways.

Mysterious Green Threads

In a patch where no one dares to tread,
Lurks a tangled mess of green instead.
Threads that giggle, weave and tease,
Tying shoes and giving knees.

A squirrel jumps, it's quite a scene,
Caught in the clutches of a leafy machine.
He battles hard, but oh what a sight,
Two paws flailing, what a funny fright!

When friends walk by, they cannot miss,
The wobbling antics of greenish bliss.
"Don't trip!" they yell with hearts so light,
As laughter erupts in that leafy fight.

So if you're brave and feel quite bold,
Tread lightly where the green strands unfold.
For in those twists, fun awaits,
In the game of life, we weave our fates.

The Shrouded Path

Down a path where shadows play,
A hearty vine blocks the way.
With a grin, it sprawls and sways,
Inviting giggles through leafy maze.

A dog dashes in chasing a ball,
But trips on threads that rise and fall.
With a yelp and a roll, what a sight to see,
A cheerful tangle, as happy as can be!

Friends take bets on who will fall,
As overgrown tricks sprout with a call.
The path unfolds with laughter high,
Underneath a watchful, jolly sky.

So take a stroll, but hold your ground,
For fun awaits where shades abound.
Journey through giggles, take a chance,
In a shrouded path where shadows dance.

Shadows Entwined

In a corner where the giggles hide,
Vines wrap secrets with playful pride.
They twist and twirl in a costume grand,
Making mischief, oh so planned.

A fox tiptoes with careful grace,
But the shadows grab him, what a race!
With a flick and a swish, he spins around,
A comical chase, on leafy ground.

Friends gather 'round for a laughing feat,
As twigs snap under hopping feet.
"I swear it's alive!" one friend declares,
As shadows giggle with secret snares.

So step with caution, but bring the fun,
In tangled antics, all is won.
For under the sprigs where laughter resides,
Are shadows entwined with joyful sides.

A Dance with the Undergrowth

In a gown of green, they twirl and spin,
With leaves for skirts, and laughter within.
The roots tap beats, the branches sway,
Throwing a party in their leafy parade.

Frogs in tuxedos, crickets on drums,
Bugs all a-buzzing in jubilant hums.
Snails do the twist, in their slow-motion game,
While shadows play tricks, but who's to blame?

A caterpillar bound, yet craving the roam,
Sips on the nectar of their leafy home.
Inviting the sun for a grand jive tonight,
In the undergrowth's joy, everything feels right.

Greenery's Lament

Oh, the woes of the plants, they're mighty and great,
Always tangled and tussled, by garden gate!
They dream of the sun, and of fancy heights,
But find themselves snagged in their leafy fights.

With tendrils outstretched, they grumble and pout,
"Caught in this mess, how'd we get left out?"
While vines weave a tale, of clumsy romance,
They giggle and wiggle, at shadows that prance.

A gentle breeze teases, they laugh in despair,
Playing tag with the wind, with no time to spare.
But oh, what a dance, in their leafy distress,
Life's tangled fun, no need to impress!

Curves of Solitude

In solitude's grip, the plants start to sway,
With curves that whisper secrets of play.
Bending and twisting, they look quite absurd,
Mocking the breeze, not a single word.

Is that a shy fern, hiding under a hat?
Or just a sweet sprout, resembling a cat?
The shadows giggle, as they prance and parade,
Through curves of green, their own masquerade.

But what's this? A bug with a flair for a dance,
He trips on a petal—oh, what a chance!
In the solitude dwells a whimsical crowd,
A hidden delight, enchanting and loud!

Threads of Mystery

In the brush where the whispers of secrets reside,
Lies a story untold, with nowhere to hide.
With threads of green glimmering 'neath the dawn,
A yarn tangled up, where the shy folks have drawn.

The gossiping thorns share tales of delight,
About weeds and their hopes—how they long for the light.
While shadows depend on their trickster ways,
To weave up the stories of whimsical days.

Like a spider spinning a web in the night,
Each branch holds a tale, each leaf takes flight.
A tapestry blushes as sunlight unveils,
The humorous lives woven in leafy details.

Entwined in Mystery

Creeping tendrils twist and turn,
In corners where the critters learn.
Whispers shared with a rustle near,
A leafy laugh that none can hear.

Tangled tales in the garden's veins,
Secret meetings when it rains.
A dance of shades, a game of peek,
With leafy hands that never speak.

Shadows stretch like a cat's sly grin,
Plotting mischief as night draws in.
In this green maze, the fun never ends,
Where every leaf has quirky friends.

Giggling vines with a wicked flair,
Spreading gossip in the cool night air.
With every twist, the antics grow,
In this cloaked world where mysteries flow.

The Shade's Emissary

In corners dark, a jester prances,
A leafy mask that cleverly glances.
With every twist, a jest unfolds,
In muted hues, its story told.

A leafy wiggle, a playful tease,
Dancing lightly in the breeze.
The guardians of the moonlit fair,
Flipping shadows with silly flair.

Gliding through the night so sway,
Mischief blooms where dreams play.
Clad in green, the trickster's wile,
Can make a frown stretch into a smile.

Chasing light, it weaves and wends,
Creating laughter that never ends.
In nature's cloak, all fun to find,
A sweet embrace for every mind.

Covered in Silence

Quiet whispers swirl around,
In leafy realms where fun is found.
A shush from a vine, a hush from a leaf,
In this realm of joyful mischief and grief.

Beneath the glow of twinkling stars,
A creeping green in pajamas of scars.
Tickling the toes of moonlit pranks,
Dodging echoes with clever flanks.

Every leaf, a quiet cheer,
Wrapping secrets far and near.
In silence, laughter finds its way,
A gentle chuckle at the break of day.

Resting snug in a veil of greens,
Where the in-between is crowned with beams.
A fun parade that silently streams,
Painting smiles in nature's dreams.

The Elusive Embrace

Wrapped around the fence post high,
A playful hug from a green guy.
In a world where chaos sways,
It wraps us all in leafy ways.

A dance of leaves, a charming spin,
Inviting laughter, dashing in.
With every swirl, a heartbeat sings,
Bringing joy that lightly clings.

Tangled in a cheeky game,
It's never quite the same old same.
In shadows deep, the fun unfurls,
With every twist, laughter twirls.

Clever capers in a playful chase,
The allure of the elusive embrace.
So join the mirth as shadows play,
For leafy jesters lead the way.

Embracing the Quiet Corners

In corners where the dust bunnies play,
The leaves do a jig, or so I say.
They twist and they turn, they dance with delight,
In their secret little world, out of sight.

With a giggle and sway, they claim their ground,
Whispering secrets in the low-tuned sound.
A sprightly affair beneath swirling air,
Who knew quiet spots could hold such flair?

They watch the world pass in a comical trance,
While others rush by, they just do the dance.
A tiptoe here, a shimmy there,
Nature's shy merry-makers, with flair!

So when you wander and feel all alone,
Look for the giggles in the green grown.
Just trust in the corners and give them a peek,
For laughter is hidden where one might not seek.

Legends of the Clinging Green

In realms where the color of green takes a stand,
Legends are born in the most peculiar land.
The tales of the tendrils, bold and quite spry,
Whisper of adventures that twirl in the sky.

They clutch at the bricks with a mischievous grin,
As if royal decrees say that they must win.
"Cling on!" they cry, with mischievous glee,
As they dangle and sway, so wild and so free.

Beware of the green that seeks to explore,
It's plotting a path right up to your door.
When you turn your back, they might take a chance,
And throw a wild party—oh, what a dance!

So if you find vines with a waggish flair,
Know they've just come from the tales lingering there.
Legends, they say, are not carved in stone,
But in leaves that giggle and humorously drone.

Beneath the Weight of Climbing Spirits

Beneath the weight where the mischief brews,
Climbers cavort in their leafy shoes.
They pull at the bricks in a lively embrace,
Whispering gossip in a frolicsome race.

With every upward stretch, they giggle and tease,
"Let's see how high we can climb with such ease!"
A playful game of hide and seek,
In the land of the green, it's the life of the cheek.

When shadows grow long and the day starts to melt,
The climbing spirits all gather and belt.
Their songs of delight ring out in pure jest,
As they shimmy and shake, these vines are the best!

So tiptoe past where the shadows might hide,
Laughter awaits, just look to the side.
For beneath the whispers of those climbing dreams,
Funny moments brew in laughter-filled streams.

Twilight's Tapestry of Nature

Twilight arrives with a wink and a nod,
The tapestry weaves where the night owls trod.
Leaves start to shimmer in the soft, blushed light,
As crickets join in for a jolly old night.

The silky green threads dance in the breeze,
With a playful shimmy and quick jangly tease.
"Come join us," they chirp, "it's a riot, a ball!"
While fireflies flicker and laugh with a call.

A quilt of colors begins to unfold,
In hues that are hearty and tales yet untold.
Nature's own laughter threads joy through the air,
In twilight's embrace, there's fun anywhere!

So when evening creeps and the sun starts to yawn,
Look for the antics, where fun is reborn.
In the quilt of the night, let your heart take flight,
For laughter is woven in each starry sight.

Whispers of Climbing Greens

In the corner of the yard, they creep,
Making plans while the garden sleeps.
"Are we a plant or a sneak in disguise?"
They giggle softly, plotting their rise.

Lurking near the fence with glee,
Whispering tales of who they'll be.
"Let's tickle the toes of the passersby,"
As they snicker and curl, oh my!

With every breeze, their secrets float,
Daring homeowners to take note.
"A green parade, let's start the show!"
They twist and turn, putting on a glow.

So if you glance at that leafy plight,
Remember, they party deep in the night.
With laughter echoing through the air,
Those climbing greens just don't have a care.

Secrets Hidden Beneath Canopy

Beneath the leaves, a meeting thrives,
A club of critters with secret lives.
"Shhh! The humans must not know,"
They laugh as they practice their shadow show.

A squirrel in a hat tells tales so grand,
Of acorns hoarded in a foreign land.
They mastermind the next big feast,\nWith nutty delights,
at least five at least!

The raccoon, sly with eyes that gleam,
Offers snacks to boost the team.
"We'll thrive in style, let's up our game!"
A witty plan that's just the same.

So if you wander close and hear a cheer,
Know it's just the mischief-makers near.
Under the branches, their giggles swell,
In their leafy realm, all's well that's well.

Night's Embrace of Twisting Vines

When day bids farewell, the fun begins,
As the tendrils shake off their daytime sins.
"Let's have a ball with the moon as a friend!"
The night creatures leap; their antics don't end.

With twirls and swirls, they start the dance,
A two-step routine with a wild romance.
"Watch me spin, while you do the twist!"
A vine jokes, but none can resist.

Around the lamppost, the shadows play,
Creating shapes in a funny ballet.
"Who knew that hanging out could be this fun?"
They chuckle in rhythm, joy is hard-won.

So, if you hear laughter that seems out of sight,
Under the stars, those vines dance with delight.
A leafy fiesta where secrets bloom,
In vine-wrapped joy, they make their room.

Veiled Life Amongst Gnarled Trees

Among the gnarled wood, whispers rise,
From a secret league beneath the skies.
"Ahoy! A new leaf has come into play!"
They chant with glee, at the end of the day.

A knotty squirrel plays king of the hill,
While the owls deliver gossip with thrill.
"Have you heard about that spiky pine?"
His tales are loaded with twists divine.

The shadows stretch, and the laughter peals,
As petals giggle, spinning absurd reels.
"Can you believe they think we're all bland?"
They toss their petals, a vibrant band.

So traipse on over, join in the fun,
Amidst the old trees, under the sun.
In their tangled lives, the humor unfurls,
A veiled life with joy, the best of their worlds.

In the Grip of Green Tendrils

In the garden where shadows lurk,
A green grip sneaks with a smirk.
It tickles the gnomes, they chuckle in fright,
"Who tied our toes? Was it you, blight?"

Ah, the creeping green plays tricks on the cat,
It dances around like a mischievous brat.
Eyes wide, tail puffed, the feline protests,
While laughter erupts from the daisies' behest.

A snail starts a race with a confused old shoe,
And the vines cheer it on, as they frolic anew.
The hedges just whisper and sway to the beat,
As the moon giggles softly, a sight rare and sweet.

At twilight, the mischief begins to unwind,
A comedy tangled, you really must find.
So bring your popcorn, and don't miss the spree,
For the garden's a stage, and the stars hold the key.

The Sighs of Unseen Life

In damp corners where secrets conspire,
Whispers of laughter rise higher and higher.
A fog rolls in with a ticklish tease,
"I bet you can't guess my fave, oh, please!"

A squirrel in a tux struts down the lane,
Holding a nut like it's a champagne.
The bushes all giggle, the breeze gives a cheer,
While crickets get ready to croon out of fear.

Mice in their bowties, ready to dance,
Invite all the beetles to join in this chance.
They spin in a circle, all giggles and grins,
As the moon winks slyly, let the fun begin!

Yet some shadowy figure, all fogged in a haze,
Wonders if it's time for a whimsical phase.
With a spring in its step, it steals a sweet sigh,
And then slips away with a nod, oh my!

Forgotten Corners of the Glen

In the old glen where the winks go to hide,
A pile of leaves sparkles with pride.
"Come dance with us!" calls a voice from the past,
And a tumbleweed giggles, spinning so fast.

Lost hats and lost socks share tales quite absurd,
Of adventures they've had, oh, have you heard?
A frog with a top hat croaks wise little quotes,
Meanwhile, the toads play poker with notes.

In the dusty old shack that creaks and it moans,
The shadows jump forth from the antique phones.
They tell of a time when the sun seemed to wink,
While teacups and saucers would nod and then clink.

As twilight descends, the mischief takes flight,
A parade of oddities, a whimsical sight.
So sneak to that corner, the glen gives a call,
For laughable secrets await one and all!

The Color of Enigma

In hues of confusion, the whispers combine,
A riddle wrapped sweetly in ivy-like twine.
With curious winks, the colors engage,
As they tango in rhythm upon a grand stage.

The yellows giggle, the blues cause a fuss,
While the reds play their trumpets, and nothing is amiss.
Whirling about with a gleeful delight,
They paint the night sky with a rainbow so bright.

"What secret is held in your vibrant mix?"
Said the shadowy figure, all dressed in a fix.
"Oh, it's laughter and joy, with a pinch of the night,
Come join in the chaos, it feels just right!"

With sparkles of mischief that scatter and play,
Mysteries giggle, then frolic away.
As the colors conspire with shadows in jest,
Let the laughter and joy be a lovely guest.

Cloaked in Nature's Grasp

In greens and browns, they play their game,
Like secret ninjas, they hide their name.
With tangled limbs and a cheeky wink,
They stretch and sway, oh, what do you think?

They giggle and chuckle as they creep along,
Mischief afoot, they're where they belong.
With tendrils that tease and leaves that flail,
Who knew the forest could get so pale?

A hush falls down, a ruckus is truce,
They dance in circles, oh, what a ruse!
With each little rustle, the creatures all sigh,
Is it a plant, or a giggling spy?

So next time you wander through curious trails,
Look closely for laughs and curious tales.
For in the wild's depths, there's mirth to be found,
A cloak made of green, where joy wears a crown.

Veiled Whispers of the Wild

In the hush of the forest, secrets unfold,
With whispers so soft, and stories retold.
A tickle of leaves, a poke from the ground,
What mischief awaits, can you hear that sound?

Among tangled greens, they twist and they jive,
The sneaky plants party, oh, how they thrive!
With laughter that bubbles and rustles that tease,
They sway to the rhythm of a gentle breeze.

Who knew that the underbrush could be sly?
Those leafy pranksters, oh my, oh my!
With a rub of their leaves and a wink of their spine,
They pull off their stunts, oh, isn't it fine?

So tiptoe through nature, with eyes open wide,
For behind every leaf is a giggle inside.
The whispers of green, with joy, they impart,
In the wild, a hidden delight plays its part.

Shadows of the Forest Floor

In the depths of the woods, where shadows do slide,
Lurk the laughing leaves, full of fun and pride.
They wiggle and giggle below the tall trees,
Playing peek-a-boo with the wandering breeze!

A chortle from ferns, a snicker from moss,
Who knew these critters would be such a boss?
With a rustle and shuffle, they plan their next jest,
Oh, nature's got jokes, and they're simply the best!

They scheme all day, making mischief with flair,
As sunlight trickles down, it's quite the affair.
For among the tall trunks, they twirl and they prance,
Inviting the world to join in their dance!

So next time you wander past shadows and fun,
Remember the giggles until day is done.
The forest floor's laughter, a secret so dear,
A world full of whimsy, just waiting right here!

The Quiet Tapestry

In quiet corners, a tapestry weaves,
With whispers of laughter caught up in leaves.
A playful ensign of nature's own jest,
Each stitch a secret where joy can rest.

With vines that embrace and branches that sway,
They plot their adventures in a mischievous way.
For the heart of the wild is a blend of cheer,
Where even the shadows have giggles to share.

A chuckle from roots, a snort from the dirt,
Creating a symphony without need for hurt.
As time ticks slowly, and moments align,
The forest reveals its laughter divine.

So come take a stroll upon nature's grand stage,
Join in the folly, let life's laughs engage.
For in this green quilt, we find joy in the seams,
Together we'll weave our delight in our dreams.

The Concealed Vine

In corners where the whispers hide,
A vine looms large, but it's shy inside.
It tickles toes of passersby,
And giggles softly, oh me, oh my!

With its leafy prickle poking fate,
It's plotting mischief, oh, isn't it great?
Snagging hats and tugging shoes,
This cheeky gremlin, how can one lose?

Shaded Reverie

Beneath the tree in dappled light,
A creeping vine prepares to bite.
Not in a scary way, but quite the fun,
With leafy laughter under the sun.

Its tendrils dance and sway about,
Causing chuckles, never a doubt.
It teases birds and tickles bees,
In this playful shade with a soft, warm breeze.

An Understory of Silence

In the quiet, where shadows dwell,
A secret vine is weaving its spell.
It tells jokes with a twirl of green,
Spreading chuckles, though rarely seen.

A smash of laughter, oh, how it plays,
In the hush of twilight, it steals the gaze.
Pranks on mushrooms, tricks on ferns,
In the silence, a joy that returns.

Whispers from the Woods

From the green depths, soft giggles rise,
As a sneaky vine plots its surprise.
It tickles the bark with a gentle tease,
Every rustle feels like a gentle breeze.

With every twist, it takes a peek,
Ready to prank, never too meek.
A leafy jester dwelling unseen,
In the forest's crown, a prankster's dream.

Underneath the Lattice

Beneath the trellis where secrets hide,
A plant whispers tales when the sun's inside.
It tickles the fence with its leafy charm,
And plots on the squirrels, but means no harm.

Its tendrils reach out like fingers in play,
Waving at passersby, come what may.
A jester in green, with a twisty grin,
It spreads silly rumors of where it's been.

The bees gather round for a gossip spree,
Swapping sweet secrets over cups of tea.
While shadows twirl close, with a wink and a nod,
Entangled they giggle, all feeling quite odd.

So here in the garden, under the sun's hat,
Lives a whimsical pact, snug as a cat.
With laughter and giggles, they share their delight,
In the dance of the greens, till day turns to night.

Green Shadows Dance

In a leafy kingdom where laughter bursts,
Green shadows cavort, as if they rehearsed.
They wiggle and jiggle, jump up and down,
With a spark of mischief, they wear a sly frown.

They play peek-a-boo with the sunbeams bright,
Doing cartwheels and flips, such a silly sight!
A serenade rustles through branches and leaves,
While frogs in the pond kiss the warm summer eves.

The whispers of nature entwine like a joke,
With a ticklish breeze that makes petals choke.
The crickets are laughing, the owls roll their eyes,
At the antics of shadows, quite witty and wise.

So come join the frolic, don't be shy or slow,
Let your feet tap the rhythm, let your spirit flow.
In the garden's embrace, you'll find glee in the trance,
Where even the shadows know how to dance!

The Secret Weaver

Among the green tendrils is a spider so sly,
With a web woven tight, she catches the eye.
Her threads are like whispers, laced with a grin,
As she spins out her stories, where chaos begins.

The sunbeams are jesters, they tickle her lace,
While the ants form a crew, keeping up the pace.
Each strand holds a secret, each knot hides a tale,
In a world full of giggles, where no one is pale.

She tugs on the vines, plays tricks on the flies,
With a wink of her tarantula eyes.
The world gets a chuckle, both grand and mundane,
As the garden confesses its silly refrain.

With dew drops for laughter and shadows for cheer,
The secret she weaves, brings the joys near.
So tiptoe through flowers, and hear her soft chime,
For nature's a jester, with humor sublime.

Grappling with the Unknown

In a tangle of leaves, where the wild things grow,
There's a riddle in green, trying hard not to show.
It sways with a giggle, it wiggles just right,
Plotting the antics for a mysterious night.

There are whispers of fortune, of laughter and fear,
A dance with the shadows, as twilight draws near.
What lurks in the dark? Is it friend or a foe?
A plot twist awaits just beyond the glow.

With a leap and a bounce, they tease and they play,
Merrily grappling with night's gentle sway.
The fireflies flicker, like stars on a string,
While the shadows chuckle at what the night brings.

So fear not the unknown, embrace the delight,
Let your heart take wings in the cool moonlight.
For within every shadow, there's fun to be found,
In the dance of the greens, let laughter abound!

Shadows of the Verdant Whisper

In the garden, a vine will creep,
Wearing leaves like a robe so deep,
Tickling the toes of every shoe,
Playing hide-and-seek with the dew.

A squirrel stops to take a glance,
At the vine's odd little dance,
It twirls and spins so carefree,
Even the sun grins, can you see?

While butterflies flutter, sipping sweet,
A nearby shadow sways on its feet,
"Is that a plant or a sneaky prank?"
Chuckling softly by the garden bank.

Giggling branches, they whisper low,
The secrets that only the shadows know,
No one knows who's the biggest tease,
The vine or the breeze that bends the leaves!

Embraced by Nature's Cloak.

A leafy coil round the post did twist,
With sunlight beaming, it can't resist,
"Hey, watch me climb!" it seems to yell,
While squirrels laugh, all under its spell.

Caterpillars in tiny hats parade,
Wobbling on branches, no need to fade,
One bumps the vine, "Oh, why the fuss?"
The vine replies, "Just join the bus!"

A rogue snail slips, causing a flop,
The vine just charms, gives a little hop,
"Come along friends, let's make some fun,
The shadows are dancing, we won't be done!"

Beneath the canopy, draped like a hug,
Nature laughs loud, gives a joyful shrug,
All things leafy, bold, and bizarre,
Under this cloak, we'll explore far.

Veils of Green Whisper

In the twilight where vines conspire,
They weave their tales, a merry choir,
Tales of mischief, shadows in tow,
Whispering secrets only they know.

A ladybug dons a polka dot dress,
While a twiggy branch tries to impress,
"Do you think I'm a tree or a snake?"
It 'slithers' away, "Oh for goodness sake!"

As crickets chirp a tune quite grand,
A wandering leaf takes a bold stand,
"I'll outshine you with my brilliant glide!"
But bumps the vine, and it's squirrelly pride.

With giggles echoing through the green,
Every shadow a little unclean,
They dance together, those leafy rascals,
In a riot of laughter, oh how it baffles!

The Lurking Vines

A vine peeks out from behind the wall,
"Hey, did you see that?" it starts to call,
A petunia snorts, "Why yes I do,
You're quite the lurking little shoe!"

With tendrils twirling around the gate,
The wallflower wonders, "Is this fate?"
"Don't you fret," the vine says with flair,
"If you were tall, you'd be quite the scare!"

A rabbit hops past, stops right in place,
"What's this jungle, a twisted race?"
Vines just snicker, embracing the game,
"Join us, dear friend, it's never the same!"

Underneath the moon, in playful gloom,
All the vines twist and expand to zoom,
With giggly shadows, they take to flight,
Lurkers of laughter, they own the night!

www.ingramcontent.com/pod-product-compliance
Lightning Source LLC
Chambersburg PA
CBHW070309120526
44590CB00017B/2598